Dirty People

A teacher's classroom untwisting the world.

MR. NATE GUNTER

Copyright © 2020 Mr. Nate Gunter

Published by TGJS Publishing

All rights reserved. This book or any portion thereof may not be reproduced or used in any manner whatsoever without the express written permission of the publisher except for the use of brief quotations in a book review.

Printed in the United States of America

First Printing, 2020

ISBN 9780578631455 (Print/Paperback)
ISBN 9780578632315 (eBook)

All rights reserved.

Updates, more books, resources, and related information available at:
www.MrNateBooks.com

DEDICATION

To the shocked students inspired to courageously reject the twisted world and lovingly entrust their life to God and the gospel. – Mr. Nate

CONTENTS

Dedication 3
Preface 1

Chapter 1 - Dirty Belief 3
Chapter 2 - Dirty Parents 6
Chapter 3 - Dirty Relatives 9
Chapter 4 - Dirty Work 12
Chapter 5 - Dirty End 18

About The Author 25

PREFACE

This book began as a website blog post series in 2010-11, and it's now available in book form and usable for students and teachers (including parents and pastors). For me, it's a tool to teach.

I'm writing as a provocative teacher and pastor to a sleeping, lost world, especially students in high school to college. And, I'm purposely using unique language used from a twisted world but also found in the Bible, which is the best mirror for the world to see what's wrong and what's right. The world tends to think they are right, truthful, loving, and clear. However, the world like our hearts are often confusing.

So how do you un-confuse people? How do you untwist twisted truth? Often the untwisting seems to be confusing and you end up saying, "Mr. Nate, you are confusing! I don't understand." I reply, "Either I'm confusing or you and this world are even more confusing. Let's then clear it up with simple and profound truth."

Remember, tangling up yarn is easy, but de-tangling it is awfully difficult and confusing. Just because something initially is difficult and seemingly confusing, doesn't mean we give up or give in. Rather, we press on to God and living for him in godliness – God at work in the world and our hearts to cleanse us from confusion, providing clarity, and inspiring conviction and courage to believe what the world says is unbelievable.

We teach in a way that trains, and we train people to trust – trusting God with their life. As such, these believers become voracious, astute, steady, stable, enduring, endearing, faithful, wise, understanding, prudent, trusted, loyal, humble, forgiving, truthful, and loving hard-working people. These people know what it means to live even to their last day believing in him, their Creator of their dirty life.

Now, enter my classroom, sit down, see the mirror, be shocked, and then get to work loving people for God and his purposes in this life. I like to say, "Let God be the telos of your life, knowing that what centers your heart will then aim and align it. We all have a telos centered heart, it's just the matter of what or who is your telos."

CHAPTER 1
dirty belief

Glaring at the students, the teacher says provocatively to begin the first morning class, "We are dirty." Students, still waking up from the misery of getting out of bed, look shockingly at each other. Whispers and chuckles quickly fill the room, with slight doubt of what the teacher just said. The teacher confidently gazes into the students eyes, ready to explain the random but profound truth.

Students think the teacher is referring to hygiene, where some students may need to brush their teeth and take more showers. Others think the teacher is referring to sinful behavior like sexual dating relationships, evil found on the internet, pictures on the desk in front of them, rumors of what friends did the night before, what lingers in their thoughts during the day, or the city and neighborhood streets parents tend not to drive their children down during the night with "dirty people."

The teacher smirked knowing the purpose of the statement "we are dirty" would provoke such reactions. But, like a defibrillator device that shocks a person's heart back to life, the teacher wanted to shock the students to think differently about life.

"Why are we dirty? We are dirty people because we come from dirt," the teacher explains. "Dirt is dirty and anything that grows out of dirt is dirty just like fruit or vegetables." The teacher continued to say that food from dirt is dirty food.

The teacher slowly paced back and forth in front of the students continuing to speak as the students inquisitively listened. "We live on dirt, eat things from the dirt, build on the dirt, cover the dirt, make things out of the dirt, and have jobs because of dirt. Just by this admission, we are dirty. I like drinking dirty water people call coffee!"

"But, more so, did mankind grow out of dirt?" The teacher's answer came from a Christian biblical worldview and knew the answer would bring truth to their day and a certain future of tomorrow.

The teacher knew that what people believe is what they will live by. Many adults think students lack a worldview, but, they do have a worldview and they live by it. The issue is not if a student has a worldview, but what informs the view. Their future resides on that belief and their present behavior flows from it. To change behavior, we must inform the belief.

The teacher knows most students' worldview originate from their experiences, relationships, culture, peers, late night conversations, bathroom talks among friends, road trip laughs, parties, sports, parents or lack thereof, any religious affiliation, long gazes into sunsets, and nighttime dreams of the future. More so, the teacher knows that when life's complexities inform their worldview, their worldview will be too complex.

With nothing simple to life and only complexities, no wonder why students are desperate for certainty and rightly so. Complexities breed confusion, confusion brings stagnation, stagnation births depression, depression freezes the mind, and when the mind is frozen, life is drained from any person. Any teacher should want their students filled with life, their minds engaged, their bodies working, and their spirits certain of the future.

Therefore, the teacher wants the students' worldview to come from something simple, stable, and never changing. What then is so simple but profound? What would not fail students? What then is beautiful and awe inspiring? What then is certain? What is hopeful? What works?

Truth.

So the teacher continued saying, "We are dirty … because our parents are dirty."

CHAPTER 2
dirty parents

Glares and snares spread across the students' faces. Their minds turn and hearts churn the teacher's statements. Questions arise, "What?" "What do you mean?" "Are you sure?" Followed by statements, "You are too confusing!" "My parents are not dirty." "I can't believe he knows my parents are dirty." But, the teacher is not concerned about their reactions but about them knowing the truth.

How could the teacher say "we are dirty because our parents are dirty?" The teacher explained, "We share the same parents but from a different time in history." The students began fidgeting in the desks because of the teacher's strange statement that seemed to bring more confusion.

The teacher continued with the smirk and the explanation saying, "If you believe in evolution or a variation of the origin of the world, then our parents were either animals or molecules. If you believe in God as the Creator, then we have come from two dirty parents."

Some students dropped their head or rolled their eyes saying, "Here we go again, he keeps talking about this God and nonsense." Other students became a little bit more intrigued by the teacher's mysterious and intriguing statements. The teacher knew the students would rather go back to sleep or stay away from a belief that would affect their entire world. Students would rather stick with a worldview that is truly unbelievable and does not work in real life.

The teacher, unmoved by some student's lack of interest, continued saying, "God made the first human man out of dirt and then breathed life into his lungs. God named the first man, Adam, which has the Hebrew meaning of earthy, from dirt, man, or mankind. Therefore, Adam was a dirty man!"

The students smirked and chuckled while responding, "I guess we are dirty!" The teacher quickly replies, "Yes, and also your mom is dirty!" The classroom filled with student's roaring shocking laughter, "Ooohhhhhhh!" The teacher smiles and laughs along with the students, knowing the cultural pun.

The teacher clarifies saying, "God created the first woman by completing the first surgery in putting Adam to sleep and removing a rib to form the first woman, Eve, which means the mother of all living. Therefore, Eve, our mom, is dirty!"

Tired student faces changed to smiles, attentiveness, and intrigue. The students enjoyed learning the truth in a different way as their confusion turned to clarity. A student asks, "But why are you saying this?"

The teacher responded gently, saying, "Because this world is more confusing than my statements to you."

"I teach to diminish confusion and bring certainty, but it's tough teaching and watching students not want to learn in this country. I am not teaching you to obtain a grade and send you off into an awesome career. I teach you to believe and believe in something greater than stuff. I teach you to believe in the truth that we are to love one another as dirty relatives!"

"As a teacher, I have two options. I can teach you to learn how to take test and get grades, or I can teach you to learn to love people by your work as God intended."

"At one time, you might have asked, 'What is this world for? What are we doing here? Who are all these people in history and now? Who are my parents? Who am I?'"

"Are we descendants of animals or dirty parents with dirty relatives?" The answer determines how we treat others. I hope you don't treat me like an animal!

CHAPTER 3
dirty relatives

The students looked like university physic students solving Einstein's mass-energy equivalence formula $E = mc^2$. Instead of freezing, they continued to press the teacher for more, asking question after question while the teacher tried to answer as quickly as they asked about life's great mysteries and dirty relatives.

The teacher continued, saying, "Think about it. If we believe we came from animals, we then believe animals are equal to humans and are to be treated alike. Many times animals are treated better than humans. In America, people have grown closer to animals than humans, believing they will comfort them throughout their years. These pets hear some of the deepest and darkest secrets of their owners. Other pets are brought closer to the skin than any human could ever come."

"Isn't that confusing?"

"We are not animals. People are not animals. Our relatives are not animals. If we truly evolved from animals, then where did the animals evolve from? If the animals came from particles, then where did the particles come from?"

"Or if evolution is true, then we are continuing to evolve into another likeness or being. Therefore, what are we evolving into? Aliens from outer-space? Also, why is there still animals if we have come from animals? Are we just co-existing with future humans?"

"I understand that many say Christianity is more confusing than any religion or belief system on the earth. According to many, the Bible is filled with an angry divine being in heaven and contains no scientific data to prove his existence. But one cannot say evolution is more believable than Christianity."

"I am left with three options."

"First, evolution is true and God is not. Second, God is true and evolution is not. Third, God made evolution."

"Since evolution bypasses the fact that God made the first parents from dirt, then the first two options remain. Then I ask myself the question, 'What's more believable, that the world's first parents were an unknown particle or the Christian's knowable God?'"

"How is evolution more believable when the educational picture charts depicting the evolutionary process were created by humans on a theoretical basis and not from reality. And, also, when for thousands of years, history contains trackable and traceable factual information that humans came from humans by conception and reproduction. We have yet to witness a mother giving birth to a zebra nor a horse birthing a young man."

"If we have evolved, then we have two options."

"First, we live in a survival of the fittest culture, where the healthy people win every time. Second, we live with no standards. In either option, why should I care for you? No reason! It is a completely selfish process. The only standard is to have no standards and survive by overpowering others by being the fittest.

"But, what if we are all dirty relatives with the same dirty parents? If they existed and God is true, then his standard of life is truth and love. That changes our worldview to love dirty people, which becomes our dirty work."

CHAPTER 4
dirty work

"Wow!" became students reactions. They began to understand the relationship between belief and behavior, knowing how people horribly treat each other. Either we lack or have love. Either we live life in confusion or in love. Truth and love bring profound clarity to life. The students became itchy to hear the teacher's coming conclusion of this intriguing rabbit trail-classroom-rant of intellectual affection.

So, the teacher began concluding to the students saying, "Think about it, dirt is truthful. We walk, live, and work on this truth. It exists. The truth is always below us, on us, in us, around us, and before us. Dirt lives without us but we cannot live without dirt. We are dependent upon dirt, though dirt is never dependent upon us. Even when we die, we end up in this truthful dirt. Dirt does not lie but is unable to love."

"This dirty truth of nature helps us to understand truths of the supernatural. God is truthful. He exists. God is not dependent upon us but we are always dependent upon him. God promises when we die we eventually and eternally end up with him. Dirt is still created stuff, and God is not created since he is timeless and eternal. God does not lie and does love."

"If we have come from dirt, then we have come from God. If we came from God, then what does he want from his dirty people? He created our dirty parents to spawn more dirty people and manage the dirt."

"Simple but so complex. Seems confusing but so clear and certain."

"God created dirty parents to multiply into dirty people spawning dirty relatives for generations to come. Part of his creation, he wanted dirty people to work. The dirty work was managing the created world around them to be a wonderful place for their dirty children."

"We were created to care for each other by and with our work, the reason for learning."

"For instance, high school relationships are entirely confusing. Friends gossip and slander each other but admit they are 'BFF's' (best friends forever). A boy cheats on a girl but says he loves her and wants her to take him back after breaking up. A gang invites boys or girls into the gang to be a family and receive protection, but first, the gang initiates them into the gang by assaulting them and then trains them to do evil against their city."

"Or, a high school student saying to the teacher that he is unable to focus on his work and unable to turn in the assignment because he has ADD (attention deficit disorder) and has a doctor's prescription for validation, but reads stacks of magazines, reads hundreds of pages in non-school books, listens to endless music, watches hours of movies, writes hundreds of lines of mobile text messages, and talks to friends eye-to-eye."

"It appears that we would rather use people rather than love them. We would rather use a teacher's grace than learn. We would rather use a girl for sexual pleasure rather than love her. We would rather gang up on a city, rather than love it. We would rather slander our friends rather than love them. And people tell me the truth is confusing?"

"Our world treats each other like animals. Even so, in the 21st century, in some parts of the world, people treat animals better than each other."

"Are we really what the world tells us we are – an animal? Human animals? If so, be a loving animal? Or go with your natural instinct and harm each other for survival?"

"What then is the purpose of your life and work? Is it to become the fittest and fastest? Is it to be the best? Is it to give up, be the lowest, and be consumed by others? Talk about a confusing worldly and Godless belief."

"Your life and work without God will be pointless and self-seeking. You will greedily see your education, grades, and any future jobs and call it 'empathetic' because you are an awesome animal kinder than the others that are hunting you."

"Christianity is a dirty belief based on old, dirty truth which teaches us to love and learn because of the dirt's source – God. He existed. He created. He used his creation, even dirt, to be the greatest artist humankind will ever know. But, hey, enjoy your selfie."

"God's intention for our dirty parents was the same for all the dirty relatives which is to worship him the Creator and not his creation. Part of that worship is working."

"Want to be lazy and procrastinate? Fine. Enjoy the animal kingdom and take some more psychotic medicine to make the end of your days mindless and heartless."

"Want to be the best or get that A+ to then get that diploma, to get that degree, to get that job, to get that career, to get that money, to get that vacation, to get that retirement, to get that better end than others? Sounds like you worked to get life instead of trusting in the Creator of life. Sounds like you worked for a god of money to love versus learned work skills to love people for God's sake."

"Spend years wasting your young life not worshipping your Creator and you will taste the universe's black hole, and I'm not referring to some phenomenon in outer-space."

"Are you as students really loving? Is your world really loving? Is the workplace after school any different? Did any of the American high school students evolve out of their behavior? Is that evolution called adulthood? Or is adults just older high school students with the ability to continue their unloving behavior."

"They say it's dog-eat-dog world out there. Well that sounds awesome. Continue doing the same thing of doing Godless work and you will fit right in. Enjoy the ribs."

Dirty People

The students become wide-eyed again processing the untwisting words of their twisted world. Some slowly look down to their desks sensing conviction to then raise their heads back up with a cleansed understanding of God's truth and their twisted world.

"You might feel a sense of dirtiness of guilt and shame fully knowing you are complicit in the world's rebellion against God. But God does not want you to live in shame, guilt, and weightiness of life. Rather, his truth is a cleanser of the mind, the heart, the soul, and the world. There's good and bad dirt in the world. Bad dirt needs to be cleansed before it bacterially rots versus gives life. Some dirt soaks in nutrients to be transformed and come alive."

"You will either live as dirty, transformed people or shameful animals consuming one another for whatever Godless reason and call it 'good.' Everyone will live to an end. What is your end look like? Before the end comes, get your work done. And, do your work for God's sake, transformed to love a dirty family in desperate and deadly need of its Creator."

One of the students asks, "Well, what are we supposed to do? No one believes like that? People hate God, don't read the Bible, never attend a church, and could care less."

The teacher sincerely responds, "Maybe fear your Creator instead of crazy, animalistic, and twisted people?"

"You are dirty people, with a dirty belief, from dirty parents, among dirty relatives, and have much dirty work to be done ... therefore, get your work done before the end comes!"

Students quickly look at each other with their heads kicking back up to a "what does that mean" moment. A student quickly raises her hand, "What end?"

CHAPTER 5
dirty end

The teacher pauses, giving a sincere glare to the students. Moments that feel long and awkward can provide quick and concreting depth to understanding. Like fishing, there's a moment to wait and a moment to hook. The moment arrives and the teacher methodically and slowly provides the answer.

"A dirty end. We all will transform physiologically into the same origin – dirt. We will have a dirty death."

"You will either have a Godless or Godly dirty death."

"Your world will say 'eat, drink, and waste your life' to avoid the depressing nature of a wasted life and a horrible end. Your heart might instinctually conclude that since there's some type of end, then why not consume the world according to your desires. But remember, some have different taste buds and what they might want to consume is not along with you but rather you. Enjoy your animal kingdom to death."

"Or, understand God's curse on the world recorded in the first book of the Bible, Genesis, as evidence to your life that there is a dirty end for everyone. Remember what it says? Something like, 'dust to dust'?"

"Want to know how God hinders evil in this so-called animal kingdom of unloving people? He does not let evil eternally reign and cleanses the world naturally just as he does spiritually. Truth reigns since God reigns."

"Natural death is the temporal curse after the blessed creation became separated from the life giving source of its Creator. Satan and mankind attempted to remove the nutrients to the dirt. God is the nutrition that gives life."

"Natural death does not show the absence of God in the world, but a taste of a loving, present, involved God showing what it would taste like to live eternally without him."

"Anyone ever ridicule God at a funeral, at least in their mind, of how a good God can let this bad death happen to a good person? Maybe there was a plan well before any of us lived. Maybe God's plan for funerals was to remember him and his truthful and cyclical promises."

"Did his word come true that we would die? Yes, his word came true. We return to dust. We are at the funeral to be reminded that we are dirty people – lifeless without him."

"Funerals are not to be celebrations of life but a moment in time to grieve what is lost, remember God's curse and promises, and be comforted by the presence of God. The world wants to avoid God, and we begin twisting even death. The greater comfort for a kid to an adult is God, especially in moments of life like a death and a funeral. And maybe kids and adults would be better off trained to have understood these truths as they grew and equipped or trained to deal with them rightly vs. training each generation to subtly reject their Creator in every moment of their life."

"You can continue to be lifeless without him for eternity, but he is merciful, forgiving, good, holy, righteous, enduring, endearing, long-suffering, gracious, faithful, trustworthy, loving, truthful, ever-present, involved, just, helpful, comforting, encouraging, teaching, preaching, revealing, and transforming."

"Why reject him? Come to him. Grieve to him. And you will find a grieving God who has never wanted sin or death. He is the Creator of life but also a just and righteous judge. And you think the funeral is your righteous soap box to stand in judgement of him?"

"You will meet the same truth soon as dust you shall return as life might seem slow for some but even living until you are 100 it will go by fast. Maybe the Bible talks about that as well. Something about the grass dying and flowers falling off? Or like vanishes like steam in the air?"

"Again, why reject him? Because it's hard? Tears? Loss? Others rejecting him? Evil? Unfinished business? Bright future? Hopes?"

"You will find no reason in this world to reject God. However, you will find all the truthful and loving reasons to trust him, even at a funeral. Don't fall into the dirty dark abyss while the light shines brightly on the path to follow away from your heart and the world's temptation to reject him."

"What is that path? What is that light? What is the epicenter of reason to believe? He has a name – Jesus."

"The one who came to the earth to eternally deal with evil. To provide life to the cursed dirt. To provide condemning judgment to the proud, hard dirt. To provide eternal wrath to Satan and his demonic followers. To provide merciful judgement to the humble, receptive dirt."

"What are you supposed to do? You can't do anything. You are dead dirt. There's no nutrition in you. You are Godless, but God promises that doesn't have to stay that way."

"He's nutritious. He's the nutrition to dying dirt. He's life giving as from the beginning in creating his dirty people. As he gives life, enjoy the fresh air of your first awakened breaths. He will form and transform you before and after your dirty death. Like a baby just born breathing, so you are when trusting in Christ with your life. Maybe Jesus mentioned something like 'born-again'?"

"And when the cursed dirty death comes and we stand at your funeral, we will not grieve hopelessly but rather trust his promises that you will have breath and life again with him and with us. We will be tearful, damp, dirty people longing to see you but fully knowing not yet. Our hope at a funeral or at any point during this life is not in life, ourselves, or our future but in the Maker and Creator of dirt."

"Don't focus on and fear the world, yourself, or your end. Focus on and fear your Creator in your youth as the old, Israel king Solomon says in the Bible's Old Testament books of Proverbs and Ecclesiastes."

"Your Creator is considered the beginning and end and the one at work in between."

"Don't be scorched earth in the end, but be resurrected life in his presence. We will smile together at him in thankfulness for his love. Until then, we live and endure for his sake which includes the difficult things of life like death."

"Maybe, just maybe, God is different from how many of our dirty relatives describe and depict him. And maybe, just maybe, he gives us life before our dirty end to love him and others. And maybe, just maybe, we will be his dirty, loving people learning skills to be at work in real life for his purposes. And maybe, just maybe, he will bring about something unique from this dirty people that's tasty like fruit to a famished dirty soul."

"When they taste of that dirty, loving fruit, they will not taste the same nasty, deadly world but his goodness and good news of truth and love inspiring them to trust him with the entirety of their life, including their end."

"They will taste purpose. They will taste love. The will taste truth. They will taste reason. They will taste stability. They will taste eternity."

"They will taste not as a predator hunting its prey in this dog-eat-dog world, but differently, as in a holy manner receiving transformative life to awe this awesome Creator God who loves you and this world through the person and work of Christ Jesus. And maybe, just maybe, that's where the Holy Spirit is at work to bring and bear Godliness in this Godless, dirty world."

"Believe him in this unbelievable world!"
"Now, are you ready to get to work today?"

ABOUT THE AUTHOR

Mr. Nate Gunter is married to Abby and they have 7 kids (4 girls and 3 boys). He grew up in the Sacramento, CA region at Valley Christian Academy (Roseville, CA). He degreed with a B.A. in Biblical Studies at The Master's University (Santa Clarita, CA) and Th.M. in Educational Leadership at Dallas Theological Seminary (Dallas, TX).

He pastors among Telos Church(es) and educating founder with Telos Center training resource. He has worked in various capacities since he was a kid, and he has experienced various jobs providing a unique perspective to real life: janitorial, construction, plumbing, athletics, food service, equestrian therapy, shipping and logistics, customer service, sales, travel, international student education, real estate, system and database development, teacher, and pastor.

He authors Mr. Nate Books, an illustrated kid's book collection along with an educational books edition.

Helpful links for more info:
MrNateBooks.com
TelosNotes.org

www.ingramcontent.com/pod-product-compliance
Lightning Source LLC
Chambersburg PA
CBHW071418290426
44108CB00014B/1874